P9-BZA-241

WIT and WISDOM for WOMEN

WIT and WISDOM for WOMEN

How to Stay on Track in These Fast Times

BARBARA JENKINS

A JANET THOMA BOOK

THOMAS NELSON PUBLISHERS
Nashville • Atlanta • London • Vancouver

Printed in the United States of America

Copyright © 1996 by Barbara Jenkins

All rights reserved. Written permission must be secured from the publisher to use or reproduce any part of this book, except for brief quotations in critical reviews or articles.

Published in Nashville, Tennessee, by Thomas Nelson, Inc., Publishers, and distributed in Canada by Word Communications, Ltd., Richmond, British Columbia.

The Bible version used in this publication is THE NEW KING JAMES VERSION. Copyright © 1979, 1980, 1982, 1990 Thomas Nelson, Inc., Publishers.

Library of Congress Cataloging-in-Publication Data

Jenkins, Barbara.
    Wit and wisdom for women : how to stay on track in these fast times / by Barbara Jenkins.
        p.   cm.
    "A Janet Thoma book."
    ISBN 0-7852-7416-2 (hc)
    1. Women—Quotations, maxims, etc. 2. Women—Quotations.
I. Title
PN6084.W6j46 1996
081'.082—dc20   95–49652
                                                                CIP

Printed in the United States of America.
1 2 3 4 5 6 — 01 00 99 98 97 96

To Rebekah,
My Daughter

As the path of your life unfolds, may wisdom guide your steps and be your companion.

ACKNOWLEDGMENTS

This is a book rooted in discovery, friendship, and of course, gender. Whenever I began to collect, write, and edit the musings in this book, I was reminded of all the women whose lives have been intermingled with mine or who have briefly crossed my path and left a lasting mark. This collection of wisdom reminds me that life is a work in progress and is made up of many parts and many people. It is safe to say that no woman is an island but rather a composite of those who have passed through and shared their passion, love, laughter, sorrow, despair, hope, agony, and ecstasy that is common to all.

The reflections in this book have also reminded me that a woman will never reach the finish line of her identity. Instead, she will continue to reinvent herself because life demands it. With the pressure to change and adjust to seasons in life, every woman must seek wisdom to stay the course, and they deserve to be acknowledged.

Several have passed on, others live far away, and some live close by. Surely, my memory bank has overlooked someone who should be acknowledged here so I must ask for forgiveness in advance.

Thank all of you for empowering me with your wisdom and providing light onto my path. The following names are listed at random: Annie Mae Crain, Viola Louise Pennell, Betty Jo Pennell, Laverne Eaker, Lillie Crain, Jan Taggart, Martha Smith, Lawanna McIver, Victoria Ann Pennell-Ross, Dot Murphy, Zephyr Fite, Mary Jenkins, Ruby Martin, Lucy Adele Ramsey, Emma Jean Vickers, Pat Golbitz, Elaine Ganick, Charlotte Byrd-Ward, Patti Thompson, Terri Baker, Pat Black, Ann Broughton, Sharon Cook, Velma Crook, Elizabeth Pool, Evelyn Franke, Brenda Hebert, Margaret Jenkins, Bobbie Hebert, Sarah Stevens, Dot Newson, Viki Mammina, Veta Sherman, all the women in my Sunday school class (Susan Liles, Sharon Dowdy, Betty Wayman, Amy Apon, Jana Whittle, Linda Wiggins and Mary Alice Kearley), Iva Mae Gibson, Debbie Gantenbien, Edwina Sergent, Sandy Campbell, Jean Wysocki, Tracy Goldsmith, Dot Hagerman, Evelyn George, Elizabeth Sherrill, Beryl Goodland, Mary Lou Koto, Ruth Ann Leach, Judith Rudderham and Catherine Marshall. Bless all of you.

CONTENTS

CONTENTS

FOREWORD

Women have always been the baby carriers, caretakers, and civilizers of society, but the greatest social changes since the origin of life are just down the road. All women, especially the younger ones, are going to need direction to keep on course. It will be easy to make wrong turns as moral fiber and social structure change in the future.

Many of the precepts you are about to read were passed on to me by women I met during three years I literally walked across America for *National Geographic* magazine, from 1976 to 1979, or they were catchwords from women I have met around the country after speaking to business, church, or civic groups. I have met thousands of women and wish I could remember the source of every witty or wise saying or the names of all those who have said great things in my presence, but I can't. You may even find something you have said written in this book. Therefore, I acknowledge most of the catchwords on these pages belong to a wide variety of unidentified women, while many of the sayings are credited to the women to whom they belong.

Shakespeare said it best: "Women are the books, the arts, the academies, that show, contain, and nourish all the world."

And he was right, even in these fast times.

A LOOK INTO
THE FUTURE

An unfamiliar woman's voice spoke on the other end of the telephone and caught me off guard: "Hello, are you Barbara Jenkins?" The question sounded official, and I wondered who was calling so early in the morning

I was already annoyed with my eleven-year-old son, Luke, who had been watching cartoons and not paying attention to the clock. He rushed to comb the cowlick in his carrot-red hair and then ran out the back door.

"Bye, Mom!" Luke shouted as he slammed the back door and ran down the hill to meet the school bus. My husband, Mike, had left for work an hour before. Luke was the last of our three children to leave for the day.

"Bye, Honey! Have a good day," my voice trailed behind him. I held a cup of hot coffee in midair to wave good-bye and then directed my attention back to the phone call. Since I was already peeved with Luke, I hoped this wasn't another salesperson from a telephone company asking me to switch my long distance service. I paused to collect my thoughts and made a mental search to link the woman's voice with a name. There was nothing familiar about it. I slowly answered, "Uh-h-h, yes-s-s. This is Barbara Jenkins."

"I'm sorry for calling so early, but my name is Veronica Fox and I'm from Financial Women International."

I swallowed a gulp of coffee, "From where?"

"Financial Women International," she answered, "Your name was recommended, and we wondered if you would be the keynote speaker at our upcoming statewide convention." She quickly explained that the members in her organization were professional bankers, C.P.A.'s, lawyers, stockbrokers, and financial planners. These were women in all fields of business and finance.

Another gulp of coffee helped me to keep from chuckling in her ear. There was no doubt in my mind she had the wrong person because my background was in the arts—photography, drama, painting, and writing books. Yes, I did a lot of public speaking, but not in this field. I was as far from her number-crunching organization of financial women as one could get. I was not the woman for the job.

But then she added, "We're looking for someone like you to speak about the creative mind and developing twenty-first century thinking."

All of a sudden my interest piqued. I began to ask questions and realize she was not expecting me to discuss accounting or price-income ratios, but to speak about creative thinking in the next century.

"So you want the women in your organization to know that traditional ways of thinking will be outdated in the next century?" I asked.

"Exactly," she answered.

"And you want me to tell them how to think creatively to meet the challenges ahead?"

"Yes, yes," she answered, "and, we feel you have the motivation and personal skills to start our conference with excitement and enthusiasm and to give advice to other women for their career paths."

Ten minutes later I hung up the telephone and poured myself a fresh cup of coffee to sip as I pondered the invitation I had just accepted. I sat at the breakfast table and thought meeting her request would take some work, but it would be fun.

Yes. I could do it.

Meanwhile, I stared out the window and watched a pair of redbirds fly down from the hillside of hardwoods that surrounded our backyard. They danced around an empty bird feeder and chattered for more seeds. Chrissy, our new Welsh corgi puppy, ran over to see why the birds were making such a fuss. She wagged her backside beneath the birds and pointed her nose upward with curiosity, and then barked puppy-style. Our other dog, a ten-year-old Welsh corgi, CoCo, looked patiently at the fluttering redbirds and the feisty puppy. Old CoCo yawned and rested his head between his paws. CoCo and Chrissy were a perfect picture of the differences between old and new.

Like millions of other working women, I dressed for work, loaded the dishwasher, and threw a pile of dirty clothes in the washing machine. Then I filled the dogs' bowls with food and the bird feeder with seeds. My mind mulled over the speaking invitation about the twenty-first century when CoCo brought me back to the present and nuzzled my leg for a pat on the head. Chrissy twisted and romped for equal attention. I petted both of them.

"See you guys later," I said as I pulled the car out of our hillside drive and off to the writing studio. I glanced back. The dogs looked lonely, and the house looked empty. Our older ranch house would rest quietly until late in the afternoon when everyone returned from school and work and there would be supper and homework, hustle and bustle, sibling arguments and television programs, and, finally, baths and bedtime.

It was clear our three growing children, Rebekah, Jed, and Luke, as well as our old dog and new puppy, were all living examples of constant, never-ending change. Life's changes and energy were everywhere. They were under our roof and in our backyard.

I drove down Franklin Road to the studio thinking how fast things were moving in the world and the mind-boggling differences between my grandmother's generation, who traveled in a covered wagon, to my cyberspace generation. I wondered what the future held for our children. What was ahead for me, as a woman, and my daughter coming after me? What about our families, careers, health issues, the economy, and our nation? What about the environment and our planet? Our planet reminded me of a spinning top, turning the earth into one global city. What would that mean? My mind asked questions I couldn't answer.

I began to research trends, study the latest reports,

and talk to professional and conventional women about the future and how women would be impacted. It seemed everything I read, from books to newspapers to magazine articles, said dramatic changes were on the horizon. And we women were in for some real jolts. All the predictions I read were either amazing, frightening, or disturbing.

In the closing years of this century, over 51 percent of the labor force will be women, and that percentage will rise in the twenty-first century. Women will become the new servant class working at low-paying jobs to meet domestic needs. Today, women and girls already make up 75 percent of those living in poverty.

There will be 40 million more people in the United States by 2010, increasing the population to 300 million and creating more strain on our already strained economy and natural resources. In only thirty-one years, there will be a growth spurt of 61.25 million people in the United States.

Our American society will organize both work and family very differently than we do now. Companies will scatter into smaller buildings away from downtown and be linked by faxes, modems, and video facilities. Already, seven million Americans work at home today, but by 2000, experts predict there will be 25 million telecommuters.

Baby busters will go bankrupt more often because of high credit card debt and poor money management skills Cash will become an endangered species because buying and selling will be done electronically.

Infant mortality in American inner cities, already comparable to Third World countries because of crime and poverty, will rise as inner cities continue to deteriorate.

The percentage of all children in this country who live with a single parent—nearly 27 percent—will rise.

The age for first marriages will rise, and American women will marry later. The median age for first marriages in the United States is 24.4 for women, an increase of three years since 1975.

The average life expectancy of women will be 100 years because of breakthroughs in genetics and healthier lifestyles. Educated and privileged women will routinely live to 120. Centenarians will be the fastest growing segment of society, and women centenarians will outnumber men.

Skilled, educated women will most often marry skilled, educated men. It will not be uncommon for their joint incomes to hit $200,000 or more. Women college graduates of tomorrow can expect seven career changes in their lifetimes.

Women will continue to die from heart attacks more than any other disease, including lung or breast cancer.

Women in America will become more efficient and materialistic, believing the more things they possess, the more successful they will be.

Virtual reality will allow women to enter new dimensions, from traveling around the planet to walking on the moon. There will be opportunities for computer links to every woman on earth. Women will find their greatest potential and opportunities in telepower.

My weeks of research finally passed, and the day came when I spoke to Financial Women International. My brain was loaded with facts and predictions about the future, but I chose to open the speech by telling adventure stories from my 3,000-mile walk across America and how life on the road and living out of a backpack and sleeping on the ground for three years had taught me to be adaptable and often resourceful. Then I shared many of the statistics I had learned about the future and offered guideposts for women moving into the future.

Like every other public speaker, I hoped the speech was successful. After the program, there was an autograph reception. At the end of the line stood a well-dressed woman who introduced herself as a bank president from Virginia and program chairwoman of the national convention.

"This is just what we needed to hear!" she exclaimed. We talked briefly about the changing roles of women, and then she asked me to consider speaking to the national convention in Seattle, Washington. I was honored.

It was that early morning phone call and Veronica Fox's challenge to think creatively about the future that planted the seed for this book. The research and preparation to speak to Financial Women International made me more aware than ever how fast things are changing and how all of us need guideposts as we move into the future.

Some of the sayings you will read may cause you to chuckle in laughter or sit up and take notice, but the intent is to offer wit and wisdom to those of us of the feminine gender and to help us stay on track in the fast, faster, and fastest times ever known to woman.

SECTION I.

Women
with Careers

You are probably a heroine and no one told you. As corporate America downsizes, millions of households struggle to survive, but women are coming to the rescue. Women are the "new American heroes." To fill in the gap to meet higher mortgages, pay living expenses, take a vacation, and save for college or retirement, women are waking up earlier to fix breakfast, stack dishes in the dishwasher, dress the kids, throw on a business suit, apply quick makeup, kiss the kids good-bye at the day-care center, and rush off to high-tech or big-business careers.

With the revolution of women entering the job market and charting new social courses, normal life has become an endless stream of work and more work. Women hurry to go to the grocery store after work, pick up the kids, drop them off at piano lessons, and arrive home in time to fix dinner, wash a load of clothes, and help with homework before bedtime. The common cry among working women today is, "There aren't enough hours in the day to do everything that needs to be done."

If you are a career woman, you must neglect a number of things in order to have your career. It may be housework. It may be home-cooked meals. Or time with the kids, recreation, or school events. It may be reading the newspaper, painting your nails, or, very likely, romance and sex. To put it simply, women are overworked and extremely tired.

Millions of working women have discovered there is no time to reflect or ponder what is happening to their health, personal lives, and family relationships as they struggle to keep up and move into the new mechanical future. The following insights remind us who we are and how to stay on track in these accelerated times.

The technology takeover in the future
will be intimidating
unless we remember machines don't laugh, cry,
love, nurture, or give birth.
Women do.

If women in the future
want to remain mentally healthy
and emotionally happy,
they must not lose their souls
to electronic machines.

Yes, it is possible to find time to relax,
read, laugh, have fun, and socialize.
Plan to do these things
because all work and no play
makes a woman mean.

The two best things
a working woman can have
are a cooperative husband
and a well-paid housekeeper.

"Don't overplan your career.
Women miss out on opportunities beneath
their noses because they've set a path
for themselves, and if something comes along
that upsets their plans,
instead of seeing it as a stumbling block,
they must ask themselves,
'How can I take advantage
of this experience?'"

Cheryl Gould, Vice President
NBC News

In the future, women will be pressured
to become
more sophisticated and quick.
Women who are not careful
will become more efficient than intimate.

"Get a fire in your belly
that will not be quenched
until you do what you want to do.
Don't let anything stand in your way.
Don't be afraid to make mistakes
and learn from them.
You can have it all if you're willing
to pay for it."

Margie Abrams, Founder
Associated Building Services
Houston, Texas

Every woman has creative power.
If she doesn't use
it in tomorrow's workplace,
she'll commit career suicide.

A woman entrepreneur
never lets reality get in the way
of a good idea.

If a woman doesn't show
self-confidence in the workplace,
her employer and customers
will view her as weak
and she will not be taken seriously.
Protect your career
and act confident,
even when you aren't.

A woman was lamenting her frustrations
over an immobile career to a friend.
She said, "I'm tired
of pounding on doors
and having them slammed
in my face.
I'm sick and tired of being outside the loop!"
Her friend said,
"Stop whining and start your own loop."

If you are in a powerful position,
ask yourself this question:
Am I here
to do the right thing
for people,
or simply to make money?
Your answer
shows who you are.

This is a warning to working women:
The workplace may be tough today,
but it will be unforgiving tomorrow.
Be prepared.

"Don't worry
about developing your career.
Worry instead
about developing the business
and taking care of your staff.
Career success will follow."

Geraldine Laybourne, President
Nickelodeon

"When women accept more
of the workload at the office,
home, and church,
men are more than willing
to let them."

Susan Liles, Sales Manager
Uarco Business Forms

To successfully blend
work and family,
you cannot do everything
that needs to be done in one day.
And that's O.K.

Women without vision
go nowhere.

We know times are changing
when women talk business,
finance, and politics,
and men exchange recipes.

Women under 40
will never get back
in retirement benefits what they are paying
in Social Security taxes.
Don't count on Social Security
to take care of you.
Plan and invest wisely, now.

American women
consume 97 percent of their income.
Learn to live below
your means and save the rest.
You will need it.

Expect recognition
from outsiders.
It's hard to be a heroine
in your office.

If you try and fail,
you need to fail
when you're old enough
to learn from the experience,
but young enough
to pull yourself up by the bootstraps
and start something new.

To master the future,
women must use
old fashioned grit
and never,
never,
never
quit.

"If you don't have genuine passion
for what you're doing,
don't do it.
Passion for your work
helps you through
the most difficult times."

Sandy Rowe, Editor
The Oregonian

This is a woman's life:
Before a career,
there's cooking and cleaning.
During a career,
there's cooking and cleaning.
After a career,
there's cooking and cleaning.

"You should make it your business
to know the leaders in your field.
People are intimidated
to call 'important people' for advice,
but I've always found them
to be helpful and generous
with their time."

Leslie Hindman, President & Host
Home and Garden Network

If you can't imagine yourself
being the president or vice president
of the company,
your imagination is underdeveloped.

Love your work,
and, if you don't,
find another job.

Women business owners
know one disgruntled customer
is one too many.

Women business owners will prosper
if they empower employees,
treat customers like they're important,
and make sure their customers
have a better experience
with them than the competition.

All goes well
for the woman
who conducts her business
fairly.

Women in middle management
wonder where
their company ship is going.
Women executives don't
because they're at the helm.

Sharp women know
how to promote themselves
without coming off as egotistical.

Stand up straight,
speak clearly,
and look people right in the eye,
especially in the presence
of male employers.

Every woman
should know as much as there is to know
about money
and how to manage it.

"Once, women took pride in their work,
but I think many of them have lost it.
There's no more inner reward
for a job well done.
Now, all people care about
is picking up their pay."

Eva Milom, Retired Secretary
Board of Education

"You've heard people say
it takes money to make money.
It also takes
a degree of success
to create more success."

Lawanna McIver
McIver Management, Dallas, Tex.

Believe in yourself,
but stay humble.

Many women fail
because they do not realize
how close they are to success,
and they give up.

Women who
stop learning and sharpening their skills
are like ripe fruit—
overlooked and tossed aside.

Women can dress for success
without
copying men.

"My role model
was a woman called E. J.
She always inspired me,
but one day
she thought she should retire
to spend more time with her husband.
By the way,
E. J. was 104 years old."

Janet Burgess, Supplier
Film costumes and props
Amazon Drygoods, Davenport, Iowa

Being a successful woman
doesn't depend
on just one event.

Women with careers
want it all.
You can have it all,
but not all at the same time.

SECTION II.

---

*Women
and Men*

Call it hokey. Call it syrupy. It's the oldest love story in the book when a woman meets a man in a crowded room and their eyes lock on each other like magnets. Invisible electricity shoots back and forth between them. Sparks fly. Her heart races and her face flushes with excitement—she is overwhelmed. He moves gallantly across the room toward her, and she knows destiny has brought them together. She has never felt like this before. She has been lonely and longed for strong arms like his to embrace her. She sighs. Could this be her knight in shining armor, the man of her dreams, who has finally appeared to take her away from the mundane to an exciting new life?

He is everything and more than she has ever imagined, and he's coming for her. Her mind fills with romance and her imagination with wedding bells. Anything this powerful must be love.

If you are a teenager, young adult, married or divorced, you have probably experienced feelings like this before. You know how it feels when your heart throbs and the attraction is overpowering. Your knees are weak, and there are butterflies in your stomach. You can't see it, smell it, or even touch it, but an invisible magnet creates a pull between two people. Like a virus, it strikes without rhyme or reason and knows no boundaries. It can be one step below heaven or terribly bitter, depending on the circumstances. However, few of us are prepared to recognize the difference between fleeting infatuation and real love.

Lasting relationships between women and men are too important to family and society to leave to chance and feelings alone. Many people confuse sexual attraction with real love, and since the divorce rate is over 50 percent, the time has come for women of all ages to become better educated about men and love. There's too much at stake to throw caution to the wind.

Here are bits of wit and wisdom from unsung women who know the exhilarating and sometimes dangerous world of male-female relationships.

Women believe
men will be more attracted to them
if they have pouty lips,
tucked tummies, silicone breasts,
tighter buttocks, vacuumed thighs,
toothpick bodies,
tinted hair, permanent eyeliner, longer lashes,
and false fingernails.
Poor guys; no wonder they're confused.

Women feel, act, and think
all at the same time,
but men don't.
Men think, act, and then feel.
Do yourself a favor
and remember these differences.

You cannot demand
that a man be in love with you.
Love is a gift
and should not
be taken for granted.

If you are a pretty or popular woman,
be prepared
for jealousy and hard feelings
from other women.

Women do themselves a favor
when they
keep their husbands first.
Even before the children.

If you are planning to marry,
do it with the belief
that there is no way out.

Lasting relationships
develop
in the light of day—
not in bed.

Too many women
marry for the wrong reasons.
Too many
marry the wrong man.

The more you get to know a man,
the more
you can judge
between what's fantasy
and what's reality.

Notice to men
about women:
There's money involved.

Millions of young women
are being raised in divorced or blended families.
Because of this,
their relationships are more complex.
Help can be found
where least expected—
from wise grandmothers.

The harder women try
to harness commitment and security from men,
the more
it will elude them.

Don't be surprised if married couples
drop you like a hot potato
if you become divorced or widowed.
Seek new friends
and a better life.
Seek and you will find.

When a single woman
encourages the affection of a married man,
she is foolish.
Pain and disappointment
are her future.
Get smart
and look for an eligible man.

"I may have made a wrong choice
marrying a man
who cheated and beat up on me,
but I made the right choice
to leave him."

Anonymous woman from Michigan

Silly and naive women
are seduced by
fast talkers and playboys.
Don't be silly or naive.

Women who wait and shop around
for a quality dress,
purse, shoes,
or man
will find the best.

"Our problem as women
is that we've been taught
there's supposed to be fireworks
in a relationship with a man.
I've discovered lasting relationships
come from being comfortable with each other.
Just be who you are."

Jan Taggart, Director
Hospice Center in Mississippi

A woman has an advantage
when a man's interest in her
is stronger
than her interest in him.
He will be motivated
to treat her right.

Women,
beware of false flattery.
Like a snake,
it's full of poison
and will hurt you.

Are you looking for a man?
Bookstores, churches, schools, community events,
libraries, and coffee shops
are good places to meet men.
Be creative and avoid pickup bars.

Dating is not a waste of time.
Every man you date
doesn't have to be the one you marry.
View each man
as a network to the next one
and enjoy the network.

Exercise daily
to turn back the clock
and look younger
for a longer time.

Three secrets to a long marriage:
Talk things out,
do more than your share,
and decide you don't want to live apart.

"Just because a woman
makes a terrible mistake in her life
doesn't mean
she is a mistake."

Victoria Pennell Ross
Illustrator

If you despise ugly or poor women,
you could be
either one
in the course of a day.

Men are like records
because they have two sides.
One side is a hit,
the other a bomb.

Is it better to marry a friend or lover?
If you must choose
between romantic chemistry or good treatment,
remember
how someone treats you daily
is more important than fireworks.

"I have learned
things often fall apart
so things can fall together."

Betty Wayman, President
Wayman & Associates

When a woman regards her mate
like a king,
he becomes a king among men.

A woman who is too quick or snappy
with her reply
can ruin everything.

"I thought it would never happen to me.
Now, I have AIDS
and am on death row.
I learned too late
that a value system in your head is not enough.
Life is God's property
and we're just leasing it while we're here."

Thirty-year-old mother of two preschoolers
Missouri

If you have lost that lovin' feelin',
it may be because
you want to recieve
rather than give.

A woman who agrees to move in with a man,
no strings attached,
will find it just as painful
and complicated
to end the relationship
as if they had been married.
Living together is self-deception.

Life with the right partner
can be heaven on earth,
but life with the wrong partner
will be hell on earth.

If you want to stay in a marriage,
get your in-laws out.

A woman can prevent her own divorce
by marrying the right partner
in the first place.

Women want to be led,
not driven.

A woman will become weak
and conflicted
if her allegiance is divided.
Stay away from affairs.

Never guess or assume you know
what a man
is thinking.

"It's hard to admit,
but most women are just one man
away from poverty."

Kay Herring
Nashville, Tennessee

Every woman
wants attention from a man.
Few think about giving it.

When both the woman and the man
make sincere emotional investments
in each other,
then their relationship will last.

A woman can keep her partner interested
when she lets him know
he is the most important person
in the world.

Truth that is shared with kindness and mercy
is better than brutal honesty.
Brutal honesty is cruel
and destroys feelings of trust and intimacy.

A wise woman
can tell the difference
between what is make-believe
and the here and now.

If you have to have everything your way,
then you are not ready
for a loving and lasting relationship.
Wait until you're more mature.

Please be patient.
It takes time
to build lasting relationships.

If your view of love
is easy come, easy go,
you will reap a lifetime
of suffering.
Real love
is not *Entertainment Tonight* or a laugh-in.
It is a sacred gift.

SECTION III.

*Women
of Adventure*

Are you in a rut? Do you feel trapped by your circumstances? Would you like to break out and do something totally new and different? Every woman feels confined at one time or another in her life. She may feel stagnant in her job, tied down to young children, locked in a bad marriage, or obligated as the caretaker of a chronically ill relative. There are many difficult circumstances that cause women to be unable to live a carefree life, and you may be in the midst of one.

There are very few women who love freedom and high adventure more than I do. I walked 3,000 miles across the United States on assignment for *National Geographic* magazine, carrying thirty-five pounds in my backpack and living out of a tent. I have watched glorious sunrises and breathtaking sunsets from open prairies to snow-capped mountain peaks. I've slept on riverbanks, under bridges, in pine-covered forests, in swamps, caves, and on top of the wind-swept Rocky Mountains so close to the stars I felt I could reach up and touch them. I've hiked through deserts and blizzards, been attacked by outlaws, fallen off cliffs, been hit by a car, rounded up hundreds of cattle on horseback, trapped alligators, lived through tornadoes, and much, much more. It took three books to tell these stories, and still many adventures were left untold.

Whenever I speak publicly, I share some of these adventure stories, and people imagine themselves on the road, away from the pressures of everyday life. They wonder what it would be like to walk fifteen miles a day, not knowing what was around the bend or beyond the next mile, where their next meal was coming from or who they might meet, or where they would sleep at night.

Since that once-in-a-lifetime walk, I have entered mainstream America and my lifestyle is probably similar to that of most women. I'm a busy wife and mother of two teenagers and an eleven-year-old. If that isn't enough, my children are in three different schools. Every day is chocked full with so many activities on a to-do list that it makes me weary. There's soccer practice, piano practice, school field trips, church youth activities, committee meetings, business lunches, housework, bills, errands, and my professional work as a writer and speaker.

Sometimes people ask, "Would you walk across America again?"

If I could go back in time, without children and mortgage payments, my answer would be a resounding yes! It was an incredible journey full of rich experiences I shall remember the rest of my life. But I'm at a new chapter in my life. New things are happening every day. To me, the world is still a big and beautiful place waiting to be explored, from lands far away to my own backyard.

As a woman of adventure, I have lived a life of extremes and know the exhilaration and pain of tent camping alongside the road in all kinds of weather to living in a nice, warm, and comfortable suburban home. And I have learned that a life of adventure is not limited by circumstances or money. Women of adventure have conquered their fates and know how to live exciting and fulfilling lives right where they are. They have learned to reinvent themselves and find creative ways to enjoy the world and their place in it. They know how to take mini-vacations, stop and smell the roses, and live fully in the moment.

Whatever the stage you find yourself, there's no reason for your days upon this earth to be humdrum and uneventful. Take these bits of wit and wisdom to heart and enter into the biggest adventure of all—life itself.

Stand before a quiet stream,
meadow of wildflowers,
or snow-peaked mountain
and let that vista work its magic
on your body and soul.

A woman of adventure
accepts the unknown.

Women can become too intent
upon their destination
and take no joy
on the road they travel.

Pile into the family car
and go find the great outdoors.

Adventure comes to the woman
who desires it faithfully enough.

Look ahead
because you can't get very far
looking in the rearview mirror.

If you wait
for perfect conditions to be adventurous,
it will never happen.

The world is too big
to be left unexplored.

Far off places may be exotic,
but there are discoveries to be made
closer to home.
Explore a radius
of one hundred miles around your hometown
and be surprised.

A main road block
between you and what you want to do
is the way you think.

You may be very smart,
but a high I.Q. will not teach you
how to live.

Don't go to your grave
without flying a kite, skipping rope,
going barefoot, catching fireflies,
and jumping in a mud puddle.
Let go and live.

Children shout, "Look, Mom!"
when they see butterflies or bumblebees
or any of the wonders of nature.
Children sound the wake-up call
to women of all generations.

Take a nap on the beach.

Listen
to the wind in the pines
and hear a woodland lullaby.

Ride high in the saddle
and look across wide open spaces.
Savor the land and sky you see.

Hold hands
with someone you love
and walk down a wooded path.

True adventure is not a packaged trip.
Adventure is
doing something unexpected.

Adventure means
you learn something new about yourself
and the world around you.

Who wants to visit
a trashed area at home or far away?
Teach your family to respect the earth.

White-tailed deer lift their heads and freeze
when they see people.
Hold your breath
and watch as long as you can
before they bolt away.

If you're awake,
you will find adventure in common things.

All of us are born
with a sense of wonder.
Keep it alive.

Our journey here on earth
is the most marvelous
of all adventures.

Watch the snow in the moonlight
dust your yard and trees
with new white over old.

Take your children
to pick strawberries one spring morning.

A woman of adventure
must experience it firsthand—
see it, smell it, feel it, hear it, and taste it.
Adventure is not watching other people on television
or in the movies.

Sit around a campfire
and let the flames warm your face.
Listen to crickets, pond frogs, hoot owls,
or other night sounds.
Then, look up into the enormous black bowl
of twinkling stars
and thank God you're alive.

There is more to adventure
than theme parks or high-rise hotels.
Hunt for secret places
where nature outshines everything man can make.

Some women say,
"Tomorrow, tomorrow."
Tomorrow may be too late
to find paradise.

Take a deep breath
and fill your lungs
with cool autumn air.
Walk upon a carpet of pine needles,
moss, or fallen leaves
and hear muffled and crunching sounds.

Feel hot sand
between your toes
and taste a salty ocean breeze.

All good adventurers
know the value of semi-aimless puttering around.
Too much structure
resembles a time clock,
and it stifles the spirit.

Go for a walk at dawn
and notice how yards and meadows glitter like dia-
monds,
afire with dew.

All the back roads to nowhere
are calling you.

Ride a bicycle and enjoy the sights,
feel the breeze,
hear the birds,
and meet people.

When you think too much
and do too little,
you never experience
deep down joy in living.

Women
who do not want to have their plans interrupted
or to be inconvenienced
miss out on life's best adventures.

Be bold and daring.
Face life and circumstances
with a fearless, dauntless spirit.

"Women who forget the little girl inside themselves
are clamoring for power
to the point they get lost along the way
and the joy goes out
of what they're trying to do.
I hope none of us ever grow up.
If we lose that child,
we lose the essence of life."

Jan Taggart
Mississippi

Houses,
buildings, cars,
planes, trains, boats, lands,
or seas cannot hold the spirit
of a woman of adventure.

SECTION IV.

Women with Character

One of the greatest women I ever met was a pioneer named Ruby Martin. She was almost seventy years old when we met on the side of a dusty road in west Texas, back when I was walking across America and thought I would fry before I made it across the state. It was one of those burning 115-degree days when she and her husband, Homer, pulled their pickup off the lonely road, stopped, and offered some cool water and an invitation to visit their wheat and cattle ranch down the road twenty miles, across a valley of canyons and breaks.

"Nothin's out here 'cept coyotes and rattlesnakes," Ruby said. "Bet you'd like a glass of cold Texas tea 'n a home cooked meal."

"Oh, yes ma'am." And that started our longlasting friendship.

Ruby Martin is a living pioneer because she traveled in a covered wagon from Oklahoma to Texas when she was a child. The oldest of thirteen children, she helped to raise her younger brothers and sisters. When she wasn't cooking, washing, canning, or cleaning, Ruby was chopping cotton, herding cattle, or hauling wheat on her father's land.

As a teenager, she worked in a small cafe until she married Homer in 1933. She and Homer have been married over sixty years and, side by side, they scratched a living out of 150 acres of red dirt. They farmed wheat and cotton and raised cattle. They are proud of their wood-frame, three-room ranch house, built with their own hands back in 1947. This is their castle, and I've never seen two people more content.

"This place is all we need. We don't need no more," Ruby said.

"You bet! We're mighty blessed!" Homer added.

Ruby stands tall and strong, like the sturdy oak tree in her backyard that has weathered too many tornadoes to remember. Her hair is short, gray, and naturally curly. Her face is etched with deep lines that tell about an unforgiving sun during all the years she worked the land. Ruby laughs easily, and her hazel eyes dance with laser sharp insight. She can spot a fool or phony a mile away. She has lived too close to the earth to be caught up in get-rich-quick schemes or smooth talkers. Without trying, this woman has taught me many lessons about character.

Ruby is a sparkling jewel in a treasure chest of seasoned women across America. You may have read about her in the popular cover story in the August 1979 *National Geographic* magazine, or in the best-selling book *The Walk West*, published by William Morrow in 1982. She and thousands of others from her generation have nuggets of wisdom to share with baby boomers, baby busters, and the X generation.

Throughout history, women with character have been the barometers of personal and social climates, and the time has come when we must stop and listen to them again. To stay on track in these fast times, we must listen to women like Ruby Martin.

A strong woman
will master
her own tragedies.

"Girl, you're going to learn
that money, big houses, and fancy cars
aren't everything.
What's important is to have love and compassion
for your fellow man.
Be more caring for other people."

Betty Pennell, Grandmother
The Ozarks of Missouri

Women who do not learn to look after themselves
are sabotaging themselves.

"You know what's wrong
with young girls today?
Dope and sex.
It gets ahold of our young people
before they know what's happening."

Ruby Martin, Rancher
West Texas

TURN OFF
the television, dishwasher, washing machine,
clothes dryer, CD player, computer, pager,
mobile telephone, and fax machine,
and listen to the quiet.
Quiet and stillness will keep you sane.

The little engine said,
" I think I can, I think I can."
The little girl said,
"I think I can, I think I can."
The little woman said,
"Wait a minute, I know I can."

Wise women
take time to think.

Women need to cry.
Like a good rain that waters the earth,
tears cleanse
and soothe the soul of a woman.

There are three types of old women:
First, the dear, sweet old ladies;
second, the hard-headed, stubborn old women;
and third, the mean, grouchy old witches.

If you speak only
about aches, pains, money problems, job problems,
and how the world mistreats you,
then one day you will discover
all your words have come true.
Learn to speak positive words
for positive results.

A woman's intuition
is right more than it's wrong.

Be cautious with secrets.
Assume no woman (or man) will keep them.

You can't change the past,
but your future is spotless.

Dwell on
the fine and good traits
of others.

"Why, my stars and garters!
A woman can start life
at fifty, sixty, seventy, or even ninety.
You just stand back and give me a chance."

Martha Lambert Smith, Retired Agent
ReMax Real Estate
Five Million Seller

A woman who has found herself
is free to help others
find themselves.

Women who smile
are prettier.

Weak women
are brash and tough and rude.
Strong women
are gentle, giving, and caring.
Most women are somewhere in between.

"With a determined mind
and trust in the Lord,
you can do anything."

Eula Savoie, Business Woman of the Year
Savoie's Pork Products—5.7 Million
Opelousas, Louisiana

Women achieve virtue slowly,
one action and decision at a time.

Women who talk all the time
never learn much.

Be careful not to reach a conclusion
about another woman
before you've spoken to her.

A self-confident woman
doesn't need to be loud, arrogant, or conceited.
She's simply comfortable
with herself
and what she's doing.

How women talk to one another
is as important
as what they talk about.

If you are of average intelligence
and have a good education
or marketable skill,
you can do anything you want.
That is, if you want.

If you're not doing
something constructive with your life,
then you're doing
something destructive.

Some women are just like . . .
so many other women.

Happy women
have a sense of wonder.

Women who supply the needs of others
will have
no lack themselves.

Listen up, honey.
It's never so bad
that it couldn't get worse.

It takes nearly half of a woman's life
to learn how to let go of it.

An angry woman
makes mistakes,
so don't operate out of anger.

Stop making excuses.
Push through your setbacks
and get up and get going.

A woman carrying a grudge
is a woman carrying poison.

Don't expect the worst to happen
or it probably will.
Instead,
expect the best
and it probably will.

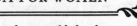

Most women suffer from self-doubt
and don't know how strong
and brave they really are.

"Real power
is being able to sit and say nothing."

Elaine Ganick, Television Producer
Ganick Communications

Women who worry
have more wrinkles.

Women avoid pain
by trying to go around it,
over it,
and under it.
The only way to stop pain
is to go through it.

Resist flattery.

A skeptical woman
says seeing is believing.
A hopeful woman
says believing is seeing.

If everything in your life is a snap,
watch out.
Nothing worthwhile
is easy to achieve.

Women who play fast and loose with principle
to make money
will lose two things:
principle and money.

SECTION V.

Women and Family

Families are not what they used to be. There was a time when we knew entire families in the neighborhood from the children to their parents and grandparents. Everyone used to have the same name but, now, no more. Today, we're lucky to know the last name of a single family member because there are likely stepparents, stepsiblings, and half-siblings, and everyone has a different last name.

Women I have met across America usually desire a nuclear family, but very few enjoy an "Ozzie and Harriet" household with a dependable father, contented mother, and playful children. Families are no longer Dad, Mom, and the kids. More than ever, modern families are blended and complex and have changed to include many different relationships of persons living together. There are childless couples, single women with children, single men with children, grandparents with grandchildren, close friends living together, and other situations where unrelated people live together, all of whom call themselves families.

There are no model families and never have been, but the historical and ideal purpose of the family was to show the nature and character of the Creator. A father and mother with children were meant to serve as a balanced picture of God's love for humankind. The father reflected God's love, guidance, authority, and protection. The mother reflected God's truth, purity, mercy, and comfort. The children reflected God's tenderness, openness, creativity, and wonder with life.

When a father, mother, and children reflect these qualities, there is a fortress of strength and protection for the family. There is security for every family member as they live and grow together. Then when the hurricanes of life rage against their wall, as they surely will, the family is able to withstand the howling winds and assaults. The family members inside know they are safe. And they know they belong.

Does anyone have a corner on the perfect family? I don't think so, but I do know the family is the closest relationship any of us can realize this side of heaven. We all struggle to learn how to love and nurture one another under our respective roofs and hope to experience a little taste of heaven here on earth. Sometimes it seems impossible, and many women give up.

Can you have a happy family? Yes, you can. It may not happen with the snap of your fingers, but a happy family is not an illusive dream. Here are bits of wisdom to help bring heaven to your family.

Do your husband and children
know you love them?
You may be surprised.

Rock your babies.
Old women knew the value
of rocking chairs
long before psychologists.

Take care of your husband
during your parenting years.
Remember,
your marriage is permanent
while parenthood is passing.

Do an extra favor
for someone in your family today.

Children are like daffodils.
Every year,
new ones keep popping up.

The first half of a woman's life
is directed by her parents.
The second half
by her children.

"Possessions are not what's important.
A broken dish isn't as important
as hurt feelings."

Lucy Adele Ramsey
Idaho

When children become adults,
they remember the little things you did together,
like playing ball, roasting marshmallows,
or hiking a trail.
They rarely remember toys.

Love looks deeper
than how your husband or children act.
Love looks to the real person.

Love your family members, wisely.

Suspicious wives
create suspicious husbands.
Suspicious parents
create suspicious children.
Create trust instead of suspicion.

Have faith in your children.
Tell them to work hard, look ahead,
and plan for the future.
And always tell them
you love them.

The mother of three quarreling children said,
"If you kids
don't learn how to get along with each other inside our
house,
how can you get along
with people out in the world?"

When you marry and have children,
make every effort
to stay married
unless there is serious abuse or adultery.
Divorce hurts everyone
and is destroying future generations.
Kids need dads.

A foolish woman
will damage her children
with too much criticism.

Praise your husband and children
over the smallest things.

Mothers should never do for their children
what their children can do
for themselves.

"There's no reason
I can't get off the fast track
and stay home with my kids,
unless I'm afraid."

Anna Quindlen, Pulitzer-Prize-winning columnist
New York Times

No woman has ever reached the end of her life
and wished she'd spent more time at the office
and less with her family.

If you must criticize your husband or children,
do it privately and not in public.

"Can you believe
it's fashionable for teenage girls
to become pregnant?
Peer pressure among teens is stronger
than parental influence.
All I can say is insist on birth control.
Don't bury your head in the sand."

Veronica Fox, V.P.
The Bank of Nashville

Women should be like owls,
always watching out
for their family.

Do you want your children
to have a sense of well-being?
Give them rules.

It's good for your mental health
when you tell your husband or children
you made a mistake.
And it's great for them.

When a child sleeps with a teddy bear or old blanket,
he is expressing his need for security.
Kiss him goodnight
and tell him everything is just fine.

Keep the husband and wife relationship
at the center of your home.
Children are more secure
when they are not on center stage.

Women are pressured
to measure up in beauty, intelligence,
and material things.
Don't pass these pressures on to your daughters.
Allow them to be themselves.

Drop whatever you are doing
and kiss your husband
when he walks in the door.

Look your child in the eye
when he wants to show you something he made at
school.
Tell him it's wonderful.

Your children
are persons who have been loaned to you
for a few short years.
They are not your possessions.

Kids are exposed to a hurricane of knowledge
too heavy for them to bear.
Kids are growing up too fast.
Pray for children.

Appreciate your husband and children's strengths
and ignore most of their weaknesses.

A self-centered child
comes from
a child-centered home.

Children need presents
on special occasions.
They need parents on all occasions.

Women suffer from the Cinderella syndrome.
They dream prince charming will take them away
and they will live happily ever after.
In the real world,
happiness can be found right where you are.

If there is verbal or sexual abuse in your family,
don't carry the pain alone.
Talk to a friend, pastor, or counselor
because there is help and healing.

What are your family traditions?
If you don't have any,
start one today.

Look at a family picture album together
and talk about grandparents,
aunts, uncles, and cousins.
Kids love it.
It helps them understand where they came from
and feel like they belong.

If you drive your children to and from school
or to various activities,
use the uninterrupted time in the car
to talk about fun or low-key things.
Don't use the time to lecture them.

Emotional safety and mutual trust
are essential to a healthy family.

Lead children to solutions to their problems.
Avoid dictating solutions.

Train your family
to eat fresh fruits, vegetables, whole wheat, and grains
and to drink lots of water.
When everyone is well,
it's easier to get along.

Read books,
poems, magazines, newspapers,
and the Bible in front of your family.
Better yet, read together.

Your family is not perfect,
and that's okay.
You're learning and growing together.
Be patient and have faith.

No matter what,
your family is worth it.

Sometimes,
troubles are so serious
all you can do is pray and wait.
Challenge your family to depend on God
because He has the answers.

SECTION VI.

Women
and Friends

I like you. Do you like me?" one little girl asked another.

"Yes, I like you. Do you like me?"

And with that simple conversation, two little girls discover the magic of friendship and begin to play patty-cake and whisper secrets.

There is an incredible power in friendship, but the fast track and mobility in our society have robbed modern women of that strength. Women need women friends, but who has the time? Dating back to childhood, women have had a gender need to share with one another from the heart. Women feel disconnected without those same close ties and confidants in adulthood.

Married women usually turn to their husbands for friendship, but before very long, they discover even the best of husbands cannot engage in "girl talk." Basic differences need to be explained to men, whereas another woman understands immediately why you want to change your hair style or go to a midnight madness sale.

When the chips are down, there's nothing like a good girlfriend. A friend is someone who accepts you—warts, wrinkles, weight, and all—unconditionally. She will listen to you cry or complain and do her best to look out for your best interests. She will cheer when you are asked to the homecoming game by the star quarterback, or she will be furious if your steady boyfriend drops you for another girl. She will be glad when you get a job promotion, or she will be sad when you don't. She supports you through thick and thin, but because there is mutual respect, she will not allow you to wallow in self-pity or manipulate her. She will encourage you to be your best self and allow you the freedom to make your own choices.

A good girlfriend is an adviser, but she is not afraid to admit her own needs or ask for help when necessary. There is a time to give advice and a time to ask for advice because friendship is a two-way street. Real friendship is reciprocal and flourishes when both parties benefit from the relationship.

All women are born with the need to communicate at a deeper level with their mothers, grandmothers, sisters, daughters, aunts, cousins, and other significant females in their lives. Wholesome friendships among women promote sound mental and emotional health. Friends remind us we are a part of something greater than ourselves, a larger world, and the right friends keep us on track. Now is the time to reclaim and reestablish ourselves as friends.

It's amazing
how every woman is full of humor,
tragedy, passionate human longings, hopes, and
fears—
if only you can unloosen the floodgates.

To have friends, be friendly.

Almost anything can happen in a day.
Who knows,
you may meet a friend
you haven't seen in years.

Rich women need friends
as well as poor women.
Too often,
rich women suffer alone
because they are too proud
to let anyone know.

The longer a woman lives,
the more *things* she can successfully live without
and continue to grow happier,
except for love, family, and *friends*.

There is a lot of human kindness
between women
once you get them together
and they discover their fears and anxieties
are not so serious after all.

Is there any better discovery
than to find out
how a woman has come to be what she is?

The best thing one woman can give to another is
the warm hand of understanding.

What a triumph
when you see an old woman
with a sunny spirit and many friends.
That's a heroic accomplishment.

A friend will remember your name.
When a friend calls your name,
it makes you feel good.

You may not have a friend
because you haven't asked for one.
"You do not have because you do not ask"
(James 4:2).

Be careful with who
you discuss your most intimate problems.
Every person cannot be trusted.
Find someone worthy of your confidence.

You were born female,
unique, irreplaceable,
and with the need to love and be loved.
Happy women *know*
they are loved by *friends* and family.

A real friend does not patronize
but offers sincere praise and encouragement.

To compliment a friend
when she has tried, yet lost,
gives her courage to keep trying
and motivation for tough times ahead.

It is important to give every woman
a chance to be a friend.

Friends are not disposable.
They should be handled with care
because friends are gifts from heaven.

Friends will not try to get ahead
at the expense of their friendship.
Instead, they replace competition
with creative interdependence.

Friendships
are living organisms at work.
They continue to unfold, change, and emerge.

No one respects a show-off or know-it-all.
If you want to have friends,
remember this.

Some women are like geodes.
They are hard to crack,
but inside,
they're full of sparkling beauty.

Nervous?
Take a deep breath,
slow down,
and call a friend.
What you are feeling
is common to all women.

Never burn your bridges.
There may come a time
when you need a friend
to help you cross back over.

If you are a woman over 40,
help younger women find their way.
Set an example
and be a friend.

Take a friend to dinner
and you will feel better.
It may surprise you
how talking to a friend over a meal
can help solve some of your problems.

Let's face it.
You will be busy forever,
so don't allow your friends
to end up at the bottom of your list.

"Don't get so upset
'cause it won't matter
a hundred years from now."

Zephyr Fite
Widow and retired farmer

When career women make friends
with other career women,
they are networking.
But when career women make friends
with poor, unfortunate women,
they are blessing themselves.

If you are not willing
to share your good fortune
with other women,
don't expect them to share your problems.

Woman, who are you?
If you really want to know,
look at the people
who love and admire you.

A friend will mold a heroine
out of a common woman.

All women need someone to listen.
Likewise,
all women need to listen.

Don't waste your time
thinking about a woman you don't like.
Instead,
love your enemy
and turn her into a friend.

There are women all around
longing for the chance
to share their troubles,
dreams, and ambitions
with someone.
Let that someone be you.

When you laugh
or cry with a friend,
she won't make fun of you.

A friend will not run
when the chips are down.

Whether a woman is young or old,
she needs a best friend.

A friend
will not force you
to change
or be someone different than you are.

Friendship does not happen by accident.
It takes time and effort
to make and keep friends.

Friends take care of what they borrow
and return it.

Friends solve their differences
without arguments
or hurtful words.

A friend
will sacrifice for you.

The joy of friendship
is found when a woman loses herself
in service to others.
To find life,
one must lose it.

Friends
have fun together.

A friend is a friend
regardless of distance or time apart.
A friend is a friend is a friend.

SECTION VII.

Women
and
Spiritual Quests

The newspaper headlines read, *"Child Killed in Gang Shooting,"* *"Teacher Shot by Angry Student,"* *"Minister Molests Young Followers,"* *"Decapitated Woman Found in Shallow Grave,"* and *"Congressman Indicted for Fraud."*

You've read these headlines before and watch the nightly news; therefore, you know great social upheaval is destroying tradition and bringing into question the most cherished beliefs and value systems practiced in this country since our founding fathers. Superficiality and emptiness have permeated our society.

There are twenty-four-hour reports about crime, war, earthquakes, starvation, lawsuits, AIDS, government fraud, and mass murderers. Then, if that isn't enough, you can watch bizarre or dysfunctional people fight and scream on various talk shows and by the end of the day, you feel depressed. If you're like me, you sometimes wonder if the whole world has gone mad. From coast to coast, there are few places to withdraw from the madness because these influences are in our living rooms.

It is true women are concerned about the upheaval in our nation and the world, but more important, they are searching for peace and security for themselves in the midst of a spinning planet and people out of control. As a result of worldwide unrest, women are turning to gurus, cults, angel worship, meditation, horoscopes, astrology, mediums, psychics, holistic diets, crystals, and other New Age practices to fill the emptiness.

However, another phenomenon is happening in America and around the globe. A great spiritual awakening is taking place among millions of Christians because of the belief that time is short before the Second Coming of Christ. Our earth and inhabitants are groaning beneath the stress of these fast times, but Christians view this time as the greatest season of spiritual harvest the world has ever known. Churches are experiencing fresh encounters with God and memberships are growing. Believers are mobilizing and infiltrating government and education to spread the gospel. Missionaries are in every remote part of the world bringing hope and compassion while local groups meet in homes to pray and help others.

Every woman is on a journey searching for answers

to her life. What is her purpose and why is she here? Life is more than the clothes a woman wears, the food she eats, the car she drives, the career she builds, the children she bears, or the house she lives in. When a woman searches for God and opens her heart's door, a miraculous thing happens. She discovers the dry, parched emptiness of her soul begins to fill with a divine dew. It's called the Spirit of God.

We are not unlike Jacob in the Old Testament who was alone on a 400-mile journey. At one point, God spoke and said, "I am with you and will watch over you wherever you go" (Gen. 28:15). Jacob was not aware that God was already with him, just as we are not aware that God is already with us. He stands at the door of every woman's heart, calling her name, before she knows it.

The beginning and ending of wisdom in our troubled times rest with the Lord, but here are heavenly tips to keep us from slipping on the fast track.

You do not have
a blackboard big enough
to draw God.

"If you start worrying
about what all is going to happen tomorrow
and in the future,
you'll go crazy.
Just put your trust in the Lord
and take it a day at a time."

Laverne Eaker
Pastor's wife in Illinois

Women who forgive others
are the ones who receive forgiveness.

A woman sees
what she looks for.

"There are only three things
I am really sure about.
There is a God,
death is no respecter of persons,
and everything changes."

Charlotte Byrd Ward, CEO
Woman of the Year, Mississippi

Dwell on the fine and good things
in another woman.
Especially,
if you think she is a jerk.

Without a purpose larger than oneself,
a woman will be empty inside.

"I think religion is necessary in life,
but probably one of our worst faults
is judging other people.
Don't you think?"

Emma Jean Vickers, Rancher
Colorado

A first-class woman
acts honorably when no one,
except God,
is looking.

Be pure.
Did you know purity
is better than power?

Women who use mystics
to find God
miss the simplicity
of being born again.

Women are in danger
when they look for guidance
from spiritual beings.
The only safe spiritual beings
are angels, and even angels must be tested.
Anything less than God Himself
can be deception.

Bless sinister people.

There are no magic tricks
to make you a contented person.
Contentment
is a by-product of hard work,
faith in God,
and love for others.

"God sometimes takes away
what seems good to us
in order to give us the best."

JoAnn Leavell, Author
New Orleans Baptist Theological Seminary

Crime happens
because of a poor pocketbook,
but more often,
crime happens because of a poor soul.

Widows, divorcees, and single women
are often very lonely.
Jesus Christ said,
"I will never leave you or forsake you."

Do you feel
tense, edgy, frustrated, confused, disappointed,
hurt, or angry?
It helps to go for a walk
and talk to God.

Poetry puts words
to the matters of your heart.
Read a poem
or Psalm every day.

The self-help, self-improvement,
and self-centered trends are dying.
Social upheaval
and difficult days ahead
will bring women out of themselves.

If you are searching for help
from a psychic,
why not bypass the interference
and go directly to God?

Someday,
women may be referred to as mere "earthlings"
in an intergalactic neighborhood.
Is this a name for creatures
so fearfully and wonderfully made in the image of
God?

"Being anxious never adds a thing,
not a single moment to a life.
Only God can cause our hearts to sing;
it's He who ends our worry and strife."

Sara Linn Richter
Teacher and Poet

After a period of searching inside oneself
for spiritual truth,
women discover "self" is not God,
but merely a vessel for His presence.

"When a woman
needs to let go of something and won't,
God knows how
to pull it out of her hands."

Carol High, Production Coordinator
REDCAP Industries

It's never too late
to choose God.

When you open your heart to God,
it's scary stuff,
but it will lead to finding your place in the world
and harmony with yourself and others.
Have courage to make the journey.

"I can't see ten years down the road,
but I believe that whatever is happening
or will happen
is where God wants me to be."

Elaine Ganick
Ganick Productions
Nashville, Tennessee

A good case of heartbreak or suffering
will awaken you out of spiritual slumber.

A regular time
of prayer and reading the Scriptures
is just as important
as toast and cereal in the morning.
They are your lifeline to spiritual survival.

When dreams
for yourself or your family
fall through and you wake up
to a reality you never expected or wanted,
say this yourself:
"This is the way it is,
but I know God still has a purpose for me."

Give of yourself every day—
a smile, hug, postcard, flowers, telephone call,
gift, letter, donation, kind word, listening ear,
or your time.
Give and your spiritual cup will be full and running
over.

When you believe tomorrow will be better,
spring is on its way,
and skies will turn blue again,
you are practicing hope.
You are also practicing faith.

Some women complain
this is a man's world
and they have little or no power.
They forget God is the source of all power.
He exalts one
and puts down another, male or female.

Why are there so many unfulfilled women?
Because as a woman thinks,
so is she.

Liberated women
are spiritually alive.

We must not place people on a pedestal.
That's known as idolatry.

A woman at peace
has stopped looking
for someone to blame.

Every woman
was born with a destiny.
Have you found yours?

Change the heart—
change the woman.

It's God's job
to make your boyfriend or husband
spiritually minded—
not yours.
Let go
and let God teach the man in your life.

God never forgets
what you do for Him.

The government is not equipped to be God.
It doesn't have the resources
to take care of the poor,
but God's churches do.

Invest in God
and your return
will be one hundredfold.

After you go to bed
and turn out the lights,
say these words:
"I've worked hard today and done my best.
Lord, please take over from here."
Then go to sleep.

FINAL PREDICTIONS

People want to know, "Is the world coming to an end?"

This is the great unsolved mystery of our time and is on the minds of people around the world and here in the United States because of how fast our world is changing. We have seen unprecedented changes in the last decade in everything from climate to technology, and people are apprehensive.

Not long ago a friend of mine stopped by to talk about a television program she had watched the night before called *Ancient Prophecies*.

Viki was disturbed after viewing the program and wanted to talk to someone. She and I had been neighbors in Nashville and had remained friends after I moved away from her neighborhood. She was a single mom who worked long hours in her photo retouching business to support her two sons, and there weren't many people to whom she could turn.

She was worried as she recounted the television program to me. She said it showed natural disasters like earthquakes, floods, famines, plagues, and terrible atrocities resulting from crime, wars, and hatred between races and nationalities of people. Sections of California and other coastal states in the West and South would no longer exist because there would be a great shift in land masses. Major cities would be destroyed by earthquakes and fall into the cavity of the earth or be under water. The television program said these events had been predicted and were being fulfilled right now, and the end of the world, as we know it, was very near.

"This is really scary to me," Viki sighed. There was despair in her voice. "A lot of these natural disasters are coming true, and I don't see much hope for America or the world. I honestly worry about the future for my kids." Her sons were about the ages of my boys.

Viki said most of the predictions quoted on television were from the Bible. Not a religious or churchgoing woman, Viki was not well versed in the Bible. It was this conversation that prompted us to talk about the future, the new millennium, and unpopular viewpoints about what was happening in the world.

"We are told in the Bible that troubling and complicated times are coming on the world." I began to tell the story about the last days as I remembered from Bible studies. I paraphrased, as best I could, what the apostles had written in the New Testament books of Luke and Acts.

There would be shocking changes way beyond the social and economic trends I had researched and mentioned in the first chapter of this book. The world's physical order would be shaken from all that had been constant and familiar.

Viki sat wide-eyed at my kitchen table. She was obviously curious because she had never heard this story before.

"You know, Viki, I've heard about the end of time all of my life from my ancestors who were country folks and farmers. They used to sit on their front porches and talk about 'The Great Tribulation.' That's what the Bible calls the last days."

Viki was fascinated but a little uncomfortable. This was heavy stuff she had never heard before. She changed the subject and reminded me of recent disasters: the worst flooding in one hundred years of the Mississippi and

Missouri rivers; earthquakes in Los Angeles, India, Japan, and Mexico City killing 25,000; hurricanes Hugo, Andrew, and Opal; and the eruption of Mount Pinatubo.

"And what about AIDS?" she asked. "If all these things are starting to happen, how much longer do you think we have?"

"No one knows, but I do know that we're not supposed to be afraid," I said. "When we see all these terrible things begin to happen, we're supposed to lift up our heads and be glad."

Viki squirmed in her chair, "Yeah, right! Glad we're goin' down."

Suddenly, it occurred to me that the television program Viki had watched about ancient prophecies dealt only with the natural ruination coming to pass on the earth and didn't tell the rest of the story. There was more than catastrophes coming to earth. The ancient prophets, like Joel, told about the coming of the Lord.

"The coming of the Lord?" Viki wondered.

"No matter how much disaster comes on earth, we don't have to be afraid. We can lift up our heads and call on the name of the Lord to save us," I told her.

Viki smiled faintly and said she had to get back to work. She had a lot to think about.

ABOUT THE AUTHOR

Barbara Jenkins is the coauthor of the international bestsellers *The Walk West* (William Morrow & Co., 1982) and *The Road Unseen* (Thomas Nelson Publishers, 1986), and the author of *I Once Knew a Woman* (Word, 1993).

She has been featured on the cover of *National Geographic* magazine and *Today's Christian Woman*. She has appeared on *Good Morning America, Focus on the Family,* CNN, and other national programs.

She currently resides in Nashville, Tennessee, with her children and husband, Mike Milom. She is working on another book and is often invited to be a motivational speaker for colleges, businesses, churches, and community groups. Her mailing address is P.O. Box 40843, Nashville, TN 37204, and her telephone number is 615-781-4965.